John Paul II's

WAY OF THE CROSS

✙ John Paul II's ✙
WAY OF THE CROSS

BOOKS & MEDIA

Boston

Library of Congress Cataloging-in-Publication Data

John Paul II, Pope, 1920–
   John Paul II's way of the cross.
     p. cm.
   ISBN 0-8198-3970-1 (pbk.)
     1. Stations of the Cross. I. Title: Way of the cross. II. Title.
   BX2040 .J64 2001
   232.96—dc21

                            00-061119

Copyright © 2000, Libreria Editrice Vaticana, Citta Del Vaticano

Printed and published in the U.S.A. by Pauline Books & Media, 50 Saint Paul's Avenue, Boston MA 02130-3491.

www.pauline.org

Pauline Books & Media is the publishing house of the Daughters of St. Paul, an international congregation of women religious serving the Church with the communications media.

2 3 4 5 6   08 07 06 05 04 03

✝

Office for the Liturgical Celebrations
of the Supreme Pontiff

Stations of the Cross at the Colosseum
Led by His Holiness
Pope John Paul II

Good Friday 2000
Holy Year

Meditations and Prayers
of His Holiness Pope John Paul II

✝

✝

Opening Prayer

The Holy Father: In the name of the Father, and of the Son, and of the Holy Spirit.

R. Amen.

"If any man would come after me, let him deny himself and take up his cross and follow me" (Mt 16:24).

Good Friday evening. For twenty centuries, the Church has gathered on this evening to remember and to relive the events of the final stage of the earthly journey of the Son of God. Once again this year, the Church in Rome meets at the Colosseum, to follow the footsteps of Jesus, who "went out, carrying his cross, to the place called The Place of the Skull, which is called in Hebrew Golgotha" (Jn 19:17).

We are here because we are convinced that the *Way of the Cross* of the Son of God was not simply a journey to the place of execution. We believe that every step of the condemned Christ, every action and every word, as well as everything felt and done

 by those who took part in this tragic drama, continues to speak to us. In his suffering and death too, Christ reveals to us the truth about God and man.

We want to concentrate on the full meaning of that event, so that what happened may speak with new power to our minds and hearts, and become the source of the grace of a real sharing in it. To share means to have a part.

What does it mean to have a part in the cross of Christ? It means to experience, in the Holy Spirit, the love hidden within the cross of Christ. It means to recognize, in the light of this love, our own cross. It means to take up that cross once more and, strengthened by this love, to continue our journey.... To journey through life, in imitation of the one who "endured the cross, despising the shame, and is seated at the right hand of the throne of God" (Heb 12:2).

Brief pause for silence.

Let us pray.

Lord Jesus Christ,
   fill our hearts with the light of your Spirit,
   so that by following you
         on your final journey
   we may come to know the price
         of our redemption
   and become worthy of a share
   in the fruits of your passion,
         death and resurrection.
You who live and reign forever and ever.

℟. Amen.

✝

Jesus is condemned to death

✝

℣. *We adore you, O Christ, and we bless you.*
℟. *Because by your holy cross*
you have redeemed the world.

"Are you the King of the Jews?" (Jn 18:33)

"My Kingdom is not of this world; if my Kingdom were of this world, my servants would fight, that I might not be handed over; but my Kingdom is not from the world" (Jn 18:36).

Pilate said to him: "So you are a king?" Jesus answered: "You say that I am a king. For this I was born, and for this I have come into the world, to bear witness to the truth. Everyone who is of the truth hears my voice." Pilate said in answer: "What is truth?"

At this point, the Roman Procurator saw no need for further questions. He went to the Jews and told them: "I find no crime in him" (cf. Jn 18:37-38).

The tragedy of Pilate is hidden in the question: *What is truth?* This was no philosophical question  about the nature of truth, but an existential question about *his own relationship with truth*. It was an attempt to escape from the voice of conscience, which was pressing him to acknowledge the truth and follow it. When someone refuses to be guided by truth, he is ultimately ready even to condemn an innocent person to death.

The accusers sense this weakness in Pilate and so do not yield. They relentlessly call for death by crucifixion. Pilate's attempts at half measures are of no avail. The cruel punishment of scourging inflicted upon the accused is not enough. When the Procurator brings Jesus, scourged and crowned with thorns, before the crowd, he seems to be looking for words, which he thinks might soften the intransigence of the mob.

Pointing to Jesus he says: *Ecce homo!* Behold the man! But the answer comes back: "Crucify him, crucify him!"

Pilate then tries to buy time: "Take him yourselves and crucify him, for I find no crime in him" (Jn 19:52-57). He is increasingly convinced that the accused is innocent, but this is not enough for him to decide in his favor.

The accusers use their final argument: "If you release this man, you are no friend of Caesar; everyone who makes himself a king sets himself against Caesar" (Jn 19:12).

This is clearly a threat. Recognizing the danger, Pilate finally gives in and pronounces the sentence. But not without the contemptuous gesture of washing his hands: "I am innocent of this...blood; see to it yourselves!" (Mt 27:24).

Thus was Jesus, the Son of the living God, the Redeemer of the world, condemned to death by crucifixion. Over the centuries, the denial of truth has spawned suffering and death. It is the innocent who pay the price of human hypocrisy. Half measures are never enough. Nor is it enough to wash one's hands. Responsibility for the blood of the just remains. This is why Christ prayed so fervently for his disciples in every age: Father, "sanctify them in the truth; your word is truth" (Jn 17:17).

Prayer

Lord Jesus Christ,
    you accepted an unjust judgment.
Grant to us
    and to all the men and women of our time
    the grace to remain faithful to the truth.
Do not allow the weight of responsibility
    for the sufferings of the innocent
    to fall upon us and upon those who come
        after us.
To you, O Jesus, just Judge,
    be honor and glory forever and ever.

℟. Amen.

All: Our Father...

Stabat Mater:

At the cross her station keeping,
     stood the mournful Mother weeping,
     close to Jesus to the last.

✟

SECOND STATION

Jesus takes up his cross

✝

℣. *We adore you, O Christ, and we bless you.*
℟. *Because by your holy cross*
   you have redeemed the world.

The cross. The instrument of a shameful death. It was not lawful to condemn a Roman citizen to death by crucifixion: it was too humiliating. The moment that Jesus of Nazareth took up the cross in order to carry it to Calvary marked a turning point in the history of the cross.

The symbol of a shameful death, reserved for the lowest classes, the cross *becomes a key.* From now on, with the help of this key, man will open the door to the deepest mystery of God. Through Christ's acceptance of the cross, the instrument of his own self-emptying, men will come to know that *God is love.* Love without limits: "God so loved the world that he gave his only Son, that whoever believes in him should not perish but have eternal life" (Jn 3:16).

This truth about God was revealed in the cross. Could it not have been revealed in some other way? Perhaps. But God *chose the cross.* The Father chose

the cross for his Son, and his Son shouldered it, carried it to Mount Calvary, and on it he offered his life.

"In the cross there is suffering, in the cross there is salvation, in the cross there is a lesson of love. O God, he who once has understood you, desires nothing else, seeks nothing else" *(Polish Lenten hymn).* The cross is the sign of a love without limits!

Prayer

Lord Jesus Christ,
    who accepted the cross at the hands of men
    to make of it the sign
    of God's saving love for humanity,
    grant us and all the men and women
        of our time

the grace of faith in this infinite love.
By passing on to the new millennium
    the sign of the cross,
    may we be authentic witnesses
    to the redemption.
To you, O Jesus, Priest and Victim,
    be praise and glory forever.

℟. *Amen.*

All: Our Father...

Stabat Mater:

Through her heart, his sorrow sharing,
    all his bitter anguish bearing,
    now at length the sword had passed.

✦

THIRD STATION

Jesus falls the first time

✝

"God laid on him the sins of us all" (cf. Is 53:6). "All we like sheep have gone astray;
   we have turned every one to his own way;
   and the Lord has laid on him
   the iniquity of us all" (Is 53:6).

Jesus falls under the cross. This will happen three times along the comparatively short stretch of the "via dolorosa." Exhaustion makes him fall. His body is stained with blood from the scourging; his head is crowned with thorns. All this causes his strength to fail. So he falls, and the weight of the cross crushes him to the ground.

We must go back to the words of the prophet, who foresaw this fall centuries earlier. It is as though he were contemplating it with his own eyes: seeing the

Servant of the Lord, on the ground under the weight of the cross, he tells us the real cause of his fall. It is this: *"God laid on him the sins of us all."*

*J*t was our sins that crushed the divine Condemned One to the ground. It was our sins that determined the weight of the cross that he carries on his shoul-ders. It was our sins that made him fall. With difficulty, Christ gets up again to continue his journey. The soldiers escorting him urge him on with shouts and blows. After a moment, the procession sets out again. Jesus falls and gets up again. In this way, the Redeemer of the world addresses in a wordless way, all those who fall. *He exhorts them to get up again.* "He himself bore our sins in his body on the wood of the cross, that we might no longer live for sin but for righteousness—by his wounds we have been healed" (cf. 1 Pt 2:24).

Prayer

O Christ,
    as you fall under the weight of our faults
    and rise again for our justification,
    we pray, help us
    and all who are weighed down by sin
    to stand up again
    and continue the journey.
Give us the strength of the Spirit
    to carry with you the cross of our weakness.
To you, O Jesus,
    crushed under the weight of our faults
    be our praise and love forever.

    ℞. *Amen.*

All: Our Father...

Stabat Mater:

Oh, how sad and sore distressed,
    was that Mother highly blessed,
    of the sole begotten One!

✝

Fourth Station

Jesus meets his Mother

✝

℣. *We adore you, O Christ, and we bless you.*
℟. *Because by your holy cross*
   you have redeemed the world.

"Do not be afraid, Mary, for you have found favor with God. And behold, you will conceive in your womb and bear a son, and you shall call his name Jesus. He will be great, and will be called the Son of the Most High; and the Lord God will give to him the throne of his father David, and he will reign over the house of Jacob forever; and his kingdom will have no end" (Lk 1:30–33).

Mary remembered these words. She often returned to them in the secret of her heart. When she met her Son on the way of the cross, perhaps these very words came to her mind with particular force: "He will reign... His kingdom will have no end," the heavenly messenger had said.

Now, as she watches her Son, condemned to death, carrying the cross on which he must die, she  might ask herself, all too humanly: So how can these words be fulfilled? In what way will he reign over the House of David? And how can it be that his kingdom will have no end? Humanly speaking, these are reasonable questions. But Mary remembered that, when she first heard the Angel's message, she had replied: "Behold, I am the handmaid of the Lord. May it be done to me according to your word" (Lk 1:38).

$\mathcal{N}$ow she sees that her word is being fulfilled as the *word of the cross*. Because she is a mother, Mary suffers deeply. But she answers now as she had answered then, at the Annunciation: *"May it be done to me according to your word."* In this way, as a mother would, she embraces the cross together with the divine Condemned One. On the way of the cross, Mary shows herself to be the mother of the Redeemer of the world. "All you who pass by the way, look and see whether there is any suffering like my suffering, which has been dealt me" (Lam 1:12). It is the Sorrowful Mother who speaks, the handmaid who is obedient to the last, the Mother of the Redeemer of the world.

Prayer

O Mary,
    who walked
    the way of the cross with your Son,
    your mother's heart torn by grief,
    but mindful always of your *fiat*
    and fully confident
        that he to whom nothing is impossible
    would be able to fulfill his promises,
    implore for us and for the generations
        yet to come
    the grace of surrender to God's love.
Help us, in the face of suffering,

rejection, and trial,
however prolonged and severe,
never to doubt his love.
To Jesus, your Son,
be honor and glory forever and ever.

℟. Amen.

All: Our Father...

Stabat Mater:

Christ above in torment hangs,
she beneath beholds the pangs,
of her dying, glorious Son.

✠

FIFTH STATION

*Simon of Cyrene
helps Jesus to carry his cross*

✝

℣. *We adore you, O Christ, and we bless you.*
℟. *Because by your holy cross*
   you have redeemed the world.

They compelled Simon (cf. Mk 15:21).

The Roman soldiers did this because they feared that in his exhaustion the Condemned Man would not be able to carry the cross as far as Golgotha. Then they would not be able to carry out the sentence of crucifixion. They were looking for someone to help carry the cross. Their eyes fell on Simon. They compelled him to take the weight upon his shoulders. We can imagine that Simon did not want to do this and objected. Carrying a cross together with a convict could be considered an act offensive to the dignity of a free man. Although unwilling, Simon took up the cross to help Jesus.

In a Lenten hymn, we hear the words: "Under the weight of the cross Jesus welcomes the Cyrenean."

These words allow us to discern a total change of perspective: the divine Condemned One is someone who, in a certain sense, *"makes a gift" of his cross.*  Was it not he who said: "He who does not take up his cross and follow me is not worthy of me" (Mt 10:38)? Simon receives a gift. *He has become "worthy" of it.* What the crowd might see as an offence to his dignity has, from the perspective of redemption, given him a new dignity. In a unique way, the Son of God has made him a sharer in his work of salvation. Is Simon aware of this?

The evangelist Mark identifies Simon of Cyrene as the "father of Alexander and Rufus" (15:21). If the sons of Simon of Cyrene were known to the first Christian community, it can be presumed that Simon too, while carrying the cross, came to believe in Christ. From being forced, he then freely accepted, as though deeply touched by the words: "Whoever does not carry his cross with me is not worthy of me." By his carrying of the cross, *Simon was brought to the knowledge of the gospel of the cross.*

Since then, this gospel has spoken to many, countless Cyreneans, called in the course of history to carry the cross with Jesus.

Prayer

O Christ,
 you gave to Simon of Cyrene
 the dignity of carrying your cross.
Welcome us too under its weight,
 welcome all men and women
 and grant to everyone the gift
  of readiness to serve.
Do not permit that we should
 turn away from those
 who are crushed by the cross of illness,
 loneliness, hunger, or injustice.
As we carry each other's burdens,
 help us to become witnesses
  to the gospel of the cross

and witnesses to you,
who live and reign forever and ever.

℟. Amen.

All: Our Father...

Stabat Mater:

Is there one who would not weep,
whelmed in miseries so deep,
Christ's dear Mother to behold?

✝

SIXTH STATION

Veronica wipes the face of Jesus

✝

℣. *We adore you, O Christ, and we bless you.*

℟. *Because by your holy cross*
you have redeemed the world.

Veronica does not appear in the Gospels. Her name is not mentioned, although the names of other women who accompanied Jesus do appear. It is possible, therefore, that the name refers more to what the woman did. In fact, according to tradition, on the road to Calvary a woman pushed her way through the soldiers escorting Jesus and with a veil wiped the sweat and blood from the Lord's face. That face remained imprinted on the veil, a faithful reflection, a *"true icon"* (*"ver-icon"*). This would be the reason for the name Veronica. If this is so, the name, which evokes the memory of what this woman did, carries with it the deepest *truth about her.*

One day, Jesus drew the criticism of onlookers when he defended a sinful woman who had poured perfumed oil on his feet and dried them with her hair. To those who objected, he replied: "Why do you trouble this woman? For she has done a beautiful thing to me.... In pouring this ointment on my body she has done it to prepare me for burial" (Mt 26:10, 12). These words could likewise be applied to Veronica.

Thus, we see the profound eloquence of this event. The Redeemer of the world presents Veronica with an authentic image of his face. The veil upon which the face of Christ remains imprinted becomes a mes-

sage for us. In a certain sense it says: This is how every act of goodness, every gesture of true love toward one's neighbor, strengthens the likeness of the Redeemer of the world in the one who acts that way. Acts of love do not pass away. Every act of goodness, of understanding, of service leaves on people's hearts an indelible imprint and makes us ever more like the One who "emptied himself, taking the form of a servant" (Phil 2:7). This is what shapes our identity and gives us our true name.

Prayer

Lord Jesus Christ,
   you accepted a woman's
   selfless gesture of love,
   and in exchange ordained
   that future generations
        should remember her
   by the name of your face.
Grant that our works
   and the works of all who will come after us
   will make us like unto you
   and will leave in the world the reflection
   of your infinite love.
To you, O Jesus,
   splendor of the Father's glory,
   be praise and glory forever.

℟. Amen.

All: Our Father...

Stabat Mater:

Can the human heart refrain,
from partaking in her pain,
in that Mother's untold pain?

Jesus falls the second time

✝

℣. *We adore you, O Christ, and we bless you.*

℟. *Because by your holy cross*
you have redeemed the world.

"I am a worm, and no man; scorned by men, and despised by the people" (Ps 22:6).

These words of the psalm come to mind as we see Jesus fall to the ground a second time under the cross. Here in the dust of the earth lies the Condemned One. Crushed by the weight of his cross, his strength drains away from him more and more. But, with great effort, he gets up again to continue his march. To us sinners, what does this second fall say? More than the first one, it seems to urge us to get up, *to get up again* on our way of the cross. Cyprian Norwid wrote: "Not behind us with the Savior's cross, but behind the Savior with our own cross." A brief saying, but one that conveys much truth. It explains how Christianity is the religion of the cross.

It tells us that every person here below meets Christ who carries the cross and falls under its

weight. In his turn, Christ, on the way to Calvary, meets every man and woman and, falling under the weight of the cross, does not cease to proclaim the good news. For two thousand years, the gospel of the cross has spoken to man. For twenty centuries Christ, getting up again from his fall, meets those who fall.

Throughout these two millennia, many people have learned that falling does not mean the end of the road. In meeting the Savior they have heard his reassuring words: "My grace is sufficient for you; for my power is made perfect in weakness" (2 Cor 12:9). Comforted, they have gotten up again and brought to the world the word of *hope, which comes from the cross.* Today, having crossed the threshold of the new millennium, we are called to penetrate more deeply the meaning of this encounter. Our generation must pass on to future centuries the good news that we are lifted up again in Christ.

Prayer

Lord Jesus Christ,
   you fall under the weight of human sin
   and you get up again in order to take it
         upon yourself and cancel it.
Give to us, weak men and women,
   the strength to carry the cross of daily life
   and to get up again from our falls,
   so that we may bring to future generations
   the Gospel of your saving power.
To you, O Jesus, our support
         when we are weak,
   be praise and glory forever.

   ℟. Amen.

All: Our Father...

Stabat Mater:

Bruised, derided, cursed, defiled,
   she beheld her tender child,
   all with bloody scourges rent.

✝

EIGHTH STATION

Jesus speaks to the women of Jerusalem

✝

℣. *We adore you, O Christ, and we bless you.*

℟. *Because by your holy cross*
you have redeemed the world.

"Daughters of Jerusalem, do not weep for me, but weep for yourselves and for your children. For behold, the days are coming when they will say, 'Blessed are the barren, and the wombs that never bore, and the breasts that never gave suck!' Then they will begin to say to the mountains, 'Fall on us'; and to the hills, 'Cover us.' For if they do this when the wood is green, what will happen when it is dry?" (Lk 23:28–31).

These are the words of Jesus to the women of Jerusalem who were weeping with compassion for the Condemned One. "Do not weep for me, but weep for yourselves and for your children." At the time, it was certainly difficult to understand the meaning of these words. They contained a prophecy that would soon come to pass. Shortly before,

Jesus had wept over Jerusalem, foretelling the terrible fate that awaited the city. Now he seems to be referring again to that fate: "Weep for your chil- dren..." Weep, because these, your very children, will be witnesses and will share in the destruction of Jerusalem, the Jerusalem which *"did not know the time of her visitation"* (cf. Lk 19:44). If, as we follow Christ on the Way of the Cross, our hearts are moved with pity for his suffering, we cannot forget that admonition.

"*For* if they do this when the wood is green, what will happen when it is dry?" For our generation, which has just left a millennium behind, rather than weep for Christ crucified, it is now the time for us to recognize *"the time of our visitation."* Already the dawn of the resurrection is shining forth. "Behold, now is the acceptable time; behold, now is the day of salvation" (2 Cor 6:2). To each of us, Christ addresses these words of the book of Revelation: "Behold, I stand at the door and knock; if anyone hears my voice and opens the door, I will come in to him and eat with him, and he with me.

He who conquers, I will grant him to sit with me on my throne, as I myself conquered and sat down with my Father on his throne" (3:20-21).

Prayer

O Christ,
    you came into this world
    to visit all those who await salvation.
Grant that our generation
    will recognize the time of its visitation
    and share in the fruits of your redemption.
Do not permit that there should be
    weeping for us
    and for the men and women
        of the third millennium
    because we have rejected
    our merciful Father's outstretched hand.
To you, O Jesus,
    born of the Virgin Daughter of Zion,
    be honor and praise forever and ever.

℞. Amen.

All: Our Father...

Stabat Mater:

> Let me share with you his pain,
> who for all my sin was slain,
> who for me in torments died.

✝

NINTH STATION

Jesus falls the third time

✝

℣. *We adore you, O Christ, and we bless you.*

℟. *Because by your holy cross*
you have redeemed the world.

Once more Christ has fallen to the ground under the weight of the cross. The crowd watches, wondering whether he will have the strength to rise again.

Saint Paul writes: "Though he was in the form of God, he did not count equality with God a thing to be grasped, but emptied himself taking the form of a servant, being born in human likeness. And being found in human form, he humbled himself and became obedient unto death, even death on a cross" (Phil 2:6-8).

The third fall seems to express just this: *the self-emptying, the kenosis of the Son of God*, his humiliation beneath the cross. Jesus had said to the disciples that he had come not to be served but to serve (cf. Mt 20:28). In the Upper Room, bending low to the ground and washing their feet, he sought, as it were, *to prepare them for this humiliation of his.* Falling to the ground for the third time on  the Way of the Cross, *he cries out loudly to us once more the mystery of himself.* Let us listen to his voice! This Condemned Man, crushed to the ground beneath the weight of the cross, now very near the place of punishment, tells us: "I am the way and the truth and the life" (Jn 14:6). "He who follows me will not walk in darkness, but will have the light of life" (Jn 8:12). Let us not be dismayed by the sight of a Condemned Man who falls to the ground exhausted under the cross. Within this outward sign of the death that is approaching, the light of life lies hidden.

Prayer

*L*ord Jesus Christ,
    through your humiliation

        beneath the cross
      you revealed to the world
            the price of its redemption.
  Grant to the men and women
            of the third millennium
      the light of faith,
      so that, as they recognize in you
      the Suffering Servant of God and man,
      they may have the courage
            to follow the same path
      which, by way of the cross
            and self-emptying,
      leads to life without end.
  To you, O Jesus, our support
            when we are weak,
      be honor and glory forever.

  ℞. *Amen.*

All: Our Father...

Stabat Mater:

  O you Mother fount of love!
  Touch my spirit from above,
      make my heart with yours accord.

✠

TENTH STATION

*Jesus is stripped and offered
gall and vinegar to drink*

✝

℣. *We adore you, O Christ, and we bless you.*

℟. *Because by your holy cross*
you have redeemed the world.

"When he tasted it, he would not drink it" (Mt 27:34).

ℋe did not want a sedative, which would have dulled his consciousness during the agony. He wanted *to be fully aware as he suffered on the cross*, accomplishing the mission he had received from the Father.

That was not what the soldiers in charge of the execution were used to. Since they had to nail a condemned man to the cross, they tried to dull his senses and his consciousness. But with Christ, this could not be. Jesus knows that his death on the cross must be a sacrifice of expiation. This is why he wants to remain alert to the very end. Without consciousness, he could not, in complete freedom, accept the *full measure of suffering*. Behold, he must mount the cross in order to offer the sacrifice of the New Covenant. He is the Priest. By means of his own blood, he must enter the eternal dwelling-places, having accomplished the world's redemption (cf. Heb 9:12).

Conscience and freedom: these are the essential elements of fully human action. The world has so  many ways of weakening the will and of darkening conscience. They must be carefully defended from all violence. Even the legitimate attempt to control pain must always be done with respect for human dignity. If life and death are to retain their true value, the depths of Christ's sacrifice must be understood, and we must unite ourselves to that sacrifice if we are to hold firm.

Prayer

Lord Jesus,
　who, with supreme dedication,
　accepted death on the cross
　　　for our salvation,
　grant to us and to all the world's people
　a share in your sacrifice on the cross,
　so that what we are and what we do
　may always be a free and conscious sharing
　in your work of salvation.
To you, O Jesus, Priest and Victim,
　be honor and glory forever.

R. Amen.

All: Our Father...

Stabat Mater:

Make me feel as you have felt,
　make my soul to glow and melt,
　with the love of Christ our Lord.

✝

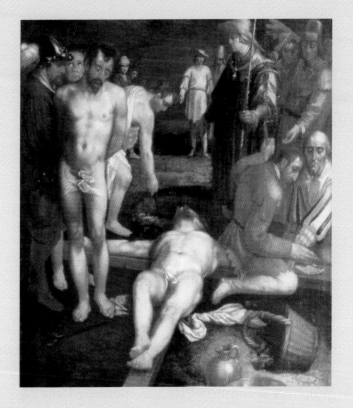

Jesus is nailed to the cross

✝

℣. *We adore you, O Christ, and we bless you.*

℟. *Because by your holy cross*
you have redeemed the world.

"They tear holes in my hands and my feet; I can count every one of my bones" (Ps 21:17‑18).

The words of the prophet are fulfilled. The execution begins. The torturers' blows crush the hands and feet of the Condemned One against the wood of the cross. The nails are driven violently into his wrists. Those nails will hold the Condemned Man as he hangs in the midst of the inexpressible torments of his agony. In his body and his supremely sensitive spirit, Christ suffers in a way beyond words. With him there are crucified two real criminals, one on his right, the other on his left. The prophecy is fulfilled: "He was numbered among the transgressors" (Is 53:12). Once the torturers raise the cross, there will begin an agony that will last three hours. This word too must be fulfilled:

"When I am lifted up from the earth, *I will draw all people to myself*" (Jn 12:32).

*W*hat is it that "draws" us to the Condemned One in agony on the cross? Certainly, the sight of such intense suffering stirs compassion. But com-passion is not enough to lead us to bind our very life to the one who hangs on the cross. How is it that, generation after generation, this appalling sight has drawn count-less hosts of people who have made the cross the hallmark of their faith? Hosts of men and women who for cen-turies have lived and given their lives looking to this sign?

From the cross, Christ draws us *by the power of love,* divine Love, which did not recoil from the to-tal gift of self; infinite Love, which on the tree of the cross, raised up from the earth the weight of Christ's body, to counterbalance the weight of the first sin; boundless Love, which has utterly filled every absence of love and allowed humanity to find refuge once more in the arms of the merciful Fa-ther. May Christ lifted high on the cross draw us, too, the men and women of the third millennium! In the shadow of the cross, let us "walk in love, as Christ loved us and gave himself up for us, a fragrant offering and sacrifice to God" (Eph 5:2).

Prayer

O Christ lifted high,
O Love crucified,
  fill our hearts with your love,
  that we may see in your cross
  the sign of our redemption
  and, drawn by your wounds
  we may live and die with you,
  who live and reign
      with the Father and the Spirit,
  now and forever.

℟. Amen.

All: Our Father...

Stabat Mater:

Holy Mother, pierce me through,
in my heart each wound renew,
of my Savior crucified.

✝

TWELFTH STATION

Jesus dies on the cross

✞

℣. *We adore you, O Christ, and we bless you.*

℟. *Because by your holy cross
you have redeemed the world.*

"Father, forgive them, for they know not what they do" (Lk 23:34).

At the height of his passion, Christ does not forget man, especially those who are directly responsible for his suffering. Jesus knows that more than anything else man needs love; he needs the mercy, which at this moment is being poured out on the world. "Truly, I say to you, today you will be with me in Paradise" (Lk 23:43). This is how Jesus replies to the plea of the criminal hanging on his right: "Jesus, remember me when you come into your kingdom" (Lk 23:42). *The promise of a new life.* This is the first fruit of the passion and imminent death of Christ. A word of hope to man. At the foot of the cross, stood Mary, and beside her the disciple, John the Evangelist. Jesus says: "Woman, behold your son!" and to the disciple: "Behold your mother!" (Jn 19:26-27). "And from that moment the disciple took her to his own home" (Jn 19:27). This is his bequest to those dearest to his heart.

His legacy to the Church. The desire of Jesus as he dies is that the maternal love of Mary should embrace all those for whom he is giving his life, the whole of humanity. Immediately after, Jesus cries out: "I am thirsty" (Jn 19:28). A word that describes the dreadful burning which consumes his whole body. It is the one word which refers directly to his physical suffering.

Then Jesus adds: "My God, my God, why have you abandoned me?" (Mt 27:46; cf. Ps 22:2). These words of the psalm are his prayer. Despite their tone, these words reveal *the depths of his union with the Father.* In the last moments of his life on earth, Jesus thinks of the Father. From this moment on, the dialogue will only be between the dying Son and the Father who accepts his sacrifice of love.

When the ninth hour comes, Jesus cries out: "It is accomplished!" (Jn 19:30). Now the work of the redemption is complete. The mission for which he came on earth has reached its goal. The rest belongs to the Father: "Father, into your hands I commit my spirit" (Lk 23:46). And having said this, he breathed his last. "The curtain of the temple was torn in two..." (Mt 27:51). The "Holy of Holies" of the Jerusalem Temple is opened at the moment when it is entered by the Priest of the New and Eternal Covenant.

Prayer

Lord Jesus Christ,
    in the moment of your agony
    you were not indifferent
        to humanity's fate,
    and with your last breath
    you entrusted to the Father's mercy

the men and women of every age,
    with all their weaknesses and sins.
Fill us and the generations yet to come
    with your Spirit of love,
    so that our indifference
    will not render vain in us
    the fruits of your death.
To you, crucified Jesus, the wisdom
       and the power of God,
    be honor and glory forever and ever.

℞. *Amen.*

All: Our Father...

Stabat Mater:

She looked upon her sweet Son,
    saw him hang in desolation,
    till his spirit forth he sent.

✠

*Jesus is taken down from the cross
and given to his Mother*

☩

℣. We adore you, O Christ, and we bless you.

℟. Because by your holy cross
you have redeemed the world.

O quam tristis et afflicta
Fuit illa benedicta
Mater Unigeniti.

In the arms of his Mother, they have placed the lifeless body of the Son. The Gospels say nothing of what she felt at that moment. It is as though by their silence the Evangelists wished to respect her sorrow, her feelings and her memories. Or that they simply felt incapable of expressing them.

It is only the devotion of the centuries that has preserved the figure of the "Pietà," providing Christian memory with the most sorrowful image of the ineffable *bond of love* which blossomed in the Mother's heart on the day of the Annunciation, and ripened as she waited for the birth of her divine Son.

That love was revealed in the cave at Bethlehem and was tested already during the presentation in the Temple. It grew deeper as Mary stored and pondered in her heart all that was happening (cf. Lk 2:51). Now this intimate bond of love must be transformed into a union, which transcends the boundary between life and death.

*A*nd thus it will be across the span of the centuries: people pause at Michelangelo's statue of the *Pietà*, they kneel before the image of the loving and sorrowful Mother *(Smetna Dobrodziejka)* in the

Church of the Franciscans in Kraków, before the Mother of the Seven Sorrows, Patroness of Slovakia; they venerate Our Lady of Sorrows in countless shrines in every part of the world. And so *they learn the difficult love* which does not flee from suffering, but surrenders trustingly to the tenderness of God, for whom nothing is impossible (cf. Lk 1:37).

Prayer

Salve, Regina, Mater misericordiæ;
  vita dulcedo et spes nostra, salve.
Ad te clamamus...
  illos tuos misericordes oculos ad nos converte
  et Iesum, benedictum fructum ventris tui,
  nobis post hoc exilium ostende.

Implore for us the grace of faith,
  hope and charity,
  so that we, like you,
  may stand without flinching
    beneath the cross
  until our last breath.
To your Son, Jesus, our Savior,
  with the Father and the Holy Spirit,
  be all honor and glory forever and ever.

℟. Amen.

All: Our Father...

Stabat Mater:

Let me mingle tears with you,
mourning him who mourned for me,
all the days that I may live.

✝

Jesus is laid in the tomb

✝

℣. *We adore you, O Christ, and we bless you.*

℟. *Because by your holy cross*
you have redeemed the world.

"He was crucified, died and was buried..."

The lifeless body of Christ has been laid in the tomb. But the stone of the tomb is not the final seal on his work. The last word belongs not to falsehood, hatred, and violence. The last word will be spoken by Love, which is stronger than death. "Unless a grain of wheat falls into the earth and dies, it remains alone; but if it dies, it bears much fruit" (Jn 12:24). The tomb is the last stage of Christ's dying through the whole course of his earthly life; *it is the sign of his supreme sacrifice* for us and for our salvation. Very soon, this tomb will become *the first proclamation of praise and exaltation of the Son of God in the glory of the Father.* "He was crucified, died and was buried...on the third day he rose from the dead." Once the lifeless body of Jesus is laid in the tomb, at the foot of Golgotha, the Church begins the vigil of Holy Saturday.

*I*n the depths of her heart, Mary stores and ponders the passion of her Son; the women agree to meet on the morning of the day after the Sabbath,  in order to anoint Christ's body with aromatic ointments; the disciples gather in the seclusion of the Upper Room, waiting for the Sabbath to pass. This vigil will end with the meeting at the tomb, the empty tomb of the Savior. Then the tomb, the silent witness of the resurrection, will speak. The stone rolled back, the inner chamber empty, the cloths on the ground—this will be what John sees when he comes to the tomb with Peter: "He saw and he believed" (Jn 20:8). And with him *the Church believed*, and from that moment she never grows weary of communicating to the world this fundamental truth of her faith: "Christ has been raised from the dead, the first fruits of those who have fallen asleep" (1 Cor 15:20). The empty tomb is *the sign of the definitive victory* of truth over falsehood, of good over evil, of mercy over sin, of life over death. The empty tomb is *the sign of the hope* which "does not deceive" (Rom 5:5). "[Our] hope is full of immortality" (cf. Wis 3:4).

Prayer

Lord Jesus Christ,
 by the power of the Holy Spirit,
 you were drawn by the Father
 from the darkness of death
 to the light of a new life in glory.
Grant that the sign of the empty tomb
 may speak to us and to future generations
 and become a wellspring of living faith,
 generous love,
 and unshakeable hope.
To you, O Jesus, whose presence,
 hidden and victorious,
 fills the history of the world,
 be honor and glory forever and ever.

℟. Amen.

All: Our Father...

Stabat Mater:

While my body here decays,
may my soul your goodness praise,
safe in paradise with you. Amen.

At the end of the Stations of the Cross, the Holy Father addressed those present:

"Was it not necessary that the Christ should suffer these things and enter into his glory?" (Lk 24:26).

℘hese words of Jesus to the two disciples on their way to Emmaus echo deep within us this evening, at the end of the Way of the Cross at the Colosseum. Like us, they had heard talk of the events surrounding the passion and crucifixion of Jesus. On the way back to their village, Christ draws near as an unknown pilgrim, and they hasten to tell him everything "about Jesus...who was a prophet mighty in deed and word before God and all the people" (Lk 24:19), and how the chief priests and rulers delivered him up to be condemned to death and how he was crucified (cf. Lk 24:20-21). And they conclude sadly: "But we had hoped that he was the one to redeem Israel. Yes, and besides all this, it is now the third day since this happened" (Lk 24:21).

"We had hoped...." The disciples are discouraged and dejected. For us too it is difficult to understand why the way of salvation should pass through suffering and death. "Was it not necessary that the Christ should suffer these things and enter into his glory?" (Lk 24:26).

ℒet us too ask this question at the end of the traditional Stations of the Cross at the Colosseum. Soon, from this place sanctified by the blood of the first martyrs, we shall go away, each on our own way. We shall return home, turning over in our minds the very same events, which the disciples of Emmaus were discussing.

May Jesus draw near to each one of us; may he become for us too a companion on the road! As he walks with us, he will explain that it was for our sake that he went to Calvary, for us that he died, in fulfillment of the Scriptures. Thus, the sorrowful event of the crucifixion, which we have just meditated upon, will become for each of us an eloquent lesson.

*D*ear Brothers and Sisters! The people of today need to meet Christ crucified and risen! Who, if not the condemned Savior, can fully understand the pain of those unjustly condemned? Who, if not the King scorned and humiliated, can meet the expectations of the countless men and women who live without hope or dignity? Who, if not the crucified Son of God, can know the sorrow and loneliness of so many lives shattered and without a future?

*T*he French poet Paul Claudel wrote that the Son of God "has shown us the way out of suffering and the possibility of its transformation" *(Positions et propositions)*. Let us open our hearts to Christ: he himself will respond to our deepest yearnings. He himself will unveil for us the mysteries of his passion and death on the cross.

"Then their eyes were opened and they recognized him" (Lk 24:31).

As Jesus speaks, the hearts of the two disconsolate travelers find a new serenity and begin to burn with joy. They recognize the Master in the breaking of bread.

Like them, may the people of today be able to recognize in the breaking of bread, in the mystery of the Eucharist, the presence of their Savior. May they encounter him in the Sacrament of his Passover, and welcome him as their fellow traveler along the way. He will listen to them and bring them comfort. He will become their guide, leading them along the paths of life toward the Father's house.

We adore you, O Christ, and we bless you,
because by your holy cross,
you have redeemed the world!

URBI ET ORBI MESSAGE
OF HIS HOLINESS POPE JOHN PAUL II

Easter Sunday, April 23, 2000

1. *"Mors et vita duello conflixere mirando..."*

"Death and life have contended
in that stupendous combat:
The Prince of life, who died,
reigns immortal" (Easter Sequence).

Once again, today, the whole Church
pauses in amazement at the empty tomb.

Like Mary Magdalen and the other women,
who came to anoint with spices
the body of the Crucified One,
like the Apostles Peter and John
who came running at the word of the women,
the Church bows before the tomb
in which her Lord was placed after the
    crucifixion.

A month ago, as a pilgrim in the Holy Land,
I had the grace of kneeling before the stone slab,
which marks the place of Jesus' burial.

Today, Easter Sunday,
I make my own the proclamation
   of the heavenly messenger:
"He is risen, he is not here" (Mk 16:6).

Yes, life and death were locked in combat
and Life was victorious forever.

All is once again oriented to life, to Eternal Life!

2. *"Victimae paschali laudes immolent christiani...."*

"Christians, to the Paschal Victim
   offer sacrifice and praise.

The sheep are ransomed by the Lamb;
and Christ, the undefiled,
has sinners to his Father reconciled."

The words of the Easter Sequence
marvelously express the mystery
accomplished in Christ's Passover.

They point to the power of renewal
flowing from his resurrection.

With the weapons of love,
God has defeated sin and death.

The Eternal Son, who emptied himself
to become the obedient servant
to the point of dying on the cross (cf. Phil 2:7-8),
has conquered evil at its roots
by opening to contrite hearts
the path of return to the Father.

He is the Gate of Life
who at Easter overcomes the gates of hell.

He is the Door of salvation, opened wide for all,
the Door of divine mercy,
who sheds a new light on human existence.

3. The Risen Christ signals the paths of hope
along which we can advance together
toward a world more just and mutually supportive,
in which the blind egoism of the few
will not prevail over the cries of pain of the many,
reducing entire peoples
to conditions of degrading misery.

May the message of life proclaimed by the angel
near the stone rolled back from the tomb
overturn the hardness of our hearts;

may it lead to removing unjustified barriers
and promote a fruitful exchange
   between peoples and cultures.

May the image of the new man,
shining on the face of Christ,
cause everyone to acknowledge
the inalienable value of human life;
may it encourage effective responses
to the increasingly felt demand
for justice and equal opportunity
   in all areas of society;
may it impel individuals and States
to full respect for the essential
   and authentic rights
rooted in the very nature of the human person.

4. *L*ord Jesus, our Peace (Eph 2:14),
Word made flesh two thousand years ago,
who by rising from the dead
   have conquered evil and sin,
grant the human family of the third millennium
a just and lasting peace;

bring to a happy outcome the talks undertaken
by people of good will who,
despite so many doubts and difficulties,
are trying to bring an end
    to the troubling conflicts in Africa,
the armed clashes
    in some countries of Latin America,
the persistent tensions affecting the Middle East,
vast areas of Asia, and some parts of Europe.

Help the nations to overcome old
    and new rivalries,
by rejecting attitudes of racism and xenophobia.

May the whole of creation,
inundated by the splendor of the resurrection,
rejoice because "the brightness of the eternal
King has vanquished the darkness of the world"
(Easter Proclamation).

Yes, Christ has risen victorious,
and has offered man, Adam's heir
    in sin and death,
a new heritage of life and glory.

5. *"Ubi est mors stimulus tuus?"*

"O death, where is your sting?" (1 Cor 15:55),
exclaims the Apostle Paul,
touched on the road to Damascus
by the light of the Risen Christ.

His cry echoes down the centuries
as the proclamation of life for the whole
of human civilization.

We too, the men and women
    of the twenty-first century,
are invited to be mindful
of this victory of Christ over death,
revealed to the women of Jerusalem
    and the Apostles,
when they arrived hesitantly at the tomb.

Through the Church, the experience
of these eyewitnesses has come down to us too.

It is a significant part
    of the journey of the pilgrims who,
during this Year of the Great Jubilee,
are entering through the Holy Door,
and going away with renewed courage

to build pathways of reconciliation with God
and with their brothers and sisters.

At the heart of this Year of grace,
may the proclamation of Christ's followers
be heard more loudly and clearly,
a joint proclamation, beyond all divisions,
in ardent longing for full communion:
"Scimus Christum surrexisse a mortuis vere."

"Yes, that Christ is truly risen
   from the dead we know,
Victorious King, your mercy show!

Tu nobis victor rex miserere." Amen.

ACKNOWLEDGEMENTS

ANDREA SOLARIO. *Christ Carrying the Cross*. Galeria
Borghese, Rome. Scala /Art Resource, NY.   *Cover (front)*

JAMES STANFIELDING / National Geographic
Society Image Collection.   *Cover (back), page* 9

GIOTTO DI BONDONE (1266–1336). *Christ before
the Sanhedrin (Jewish council)*. Scrovegni Chapel,
Padua, Italy. Alinari / Art Resource, NY.   *page* 13

RIDOLFO GHIRLANDAIO. *The Procession to Calvary*.
Copyright © National Gallery, London.   *page* 19

GIOVANNI BATTISTE TIEPOLO (1696–1770). *The Bearing
of the Cross*, c. 1738. Staatliche Museen zu Berlin–
Preußischer Kulturbesitz Gemäldegalerie.   *page* 23

FRA ANGELICO. *Christ on the Way to Calvary* from the *Armadio
degli Argenti*. Museo di San Marco, Florence, Italy.
Nicolo Orsi Battaglini / Art Resource, NY.   *page* 27

TIZIANO, 1560. *Jesús y el Cirineo*. Derechos reservados
© Museo Nacional del Prado, Madrid.   *page* 33

EL GRECO (1541–1614). *Saint Veronica with the Sudarium*.
Canvas. Museo de Santa Cruz, Toledo, Spain.
Eric Lessing / Art Resource, NY.   *page* 39

GIOVAN FRANCESCO DA MAINERI, Italian (Lombardi),
d. 1504/5. *Christ Carrying the Cross*.
Galleria Doria Pamphilj, Rome.   *page* 45

SIMONE MARTINI (1284–1344). *Christ Carrying the Cross*.
Louvre, Paris, France.
Erich Lessing / Art Resource, NY.   *page* 49

auline
BOOKS & MEDIA

The Daughters of St. Paul operate book and media centers at the following addresses. Visit, call or write the one nearest you today, or find us on the World Wide Web, www.pauline.org

CALIFORNIA
3908 Sepulveda Blvd, Culver City, CA
  90230   310-397-8676
5945 Balboa Avenue, San Diego, CA
  92111   858-565-9181
46 Geary Street, San Francisco, CA
  94108   415-781-5180
FLORIDA
145 S.W. 107th Avenue, Miami, FL
  33174   305-559-6715
HAWAII
1143 Bishop Street, Honolulu, HI
  96813   808-521-2731
Neighbor Islands call: 800-259-8463
ILLINOIS
172 North Michigan Avenue,
  Chicago, IL 60601
  312-346-4228
LOUISIANA
4403 Veterans Blvd, Metairie, LA
  70006   504-887-7631
MASSACHUSETTS
885 Providence Hwy,
  Dedham, MA 02026
  781-326-5385
MISSOURI
9804 Watson Road,
  St. Louis, MO 63126
  314-965-3512

NEW JERSEY
561 U.S. Route 1, Wick Plaza,
  Edison, NJ 08817
  732-572-1200
NEW YORK
150 East 52nd Street, New York, NY
  10022   212-754-1110
78 Fort Place, Staten Island, NY
  10301   718-447-5071
PENNSYLVANIA
9171-A Roosevelt Blvd, Philadelphia,
  PA 19114   215-676-9494
SOUTH CAROLINA
243 King Street, Charleston, SC
  29401   843-577-0175
TENNESSEE
4811 Poplar Avenue, Memphis, TN
  38117   901-761-2987
TEXAS
114 Main Plaza, San Antonio, TX
  78205   210-224-8101
VIRGINIA
1025 King Street, Alexandria, VA
  22314   703-549-3806
CANADA
3022 Dufferin Street, Toronto, Ontario,
  Canada M6B 3T5   416-781-9131
1155 Yonge Street, Toronto, Ontario,
  Canada M4T 1W2   416-934-3440

¡También somos su fuente para libros, videos y música en español!